Everything You Need to Know About

SPORTS
INJURIES

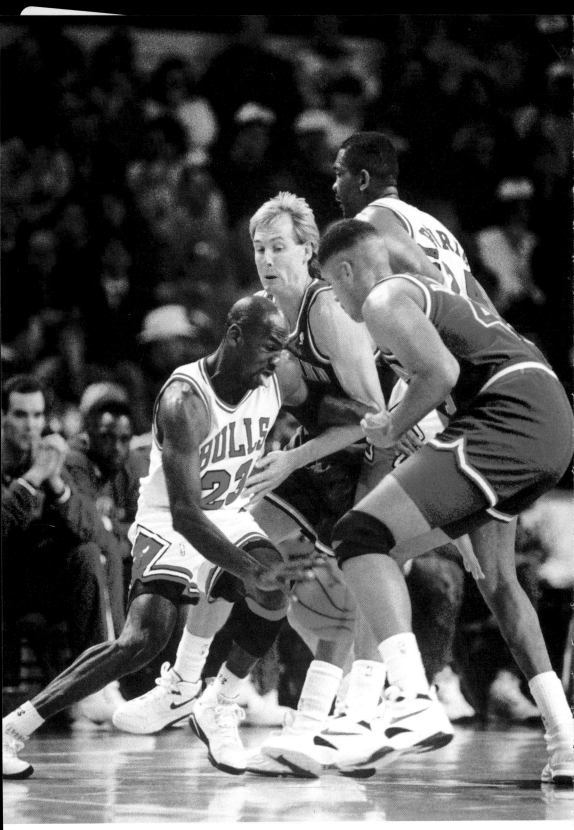

Professional athletes condition their bodies to avoid sports injuries.

Everything You Need to Know About

SPORTS INJURIES

Lawrence Clayton, Ph.D.

THE ROSEN PUBLISHING GROUP, INC.
NEW YORK

Published in 1995, 1999 by The Rosen Publishing Group, Inc.
29 East 21st Street, New York, NY 10010

Revised Edition 1999

Library of Congress Cataloging-in-Publication Data

Clayton, L. (Lawrence)
    Everything you need to know about sports injuries / Lawrence Clayton.
        p. cm. — (The Need to know library)
    Includes bibliographical references and index.
    ISBN 0-8239-2875-6
    1. Sports injuries—Juvenile literature. [1. Sports injuries.] I. Title. II. Series.
RD97.C583 1995
617.1'027—dc20
                                      94-26983
                                            CIP
                                            AC

Manufactured in the United States of America

Contents

1. How Dangerous Is Your Sport?   7

2. Head Injuries   12

3. Neck Injuries   17

4. Back Injuries   20

5. Arm, Shoulder, and Hand Injuries   28

6. Leg and Knee Injuries   35

7. Hernias   46

8. Preventing Sports Injuries   48

   Glossary   58

   Where to Go for Help   61

   For Further Reading   62

   Index   63

Nearly everyone suffers some sort of physical injury from playing sports.

Chapter 1

How Dangerous Is Your Sport?

Remember the first day you went out for football—or track or baseball, swimming or tennis? There was one thing on your mind, and it wasn't getting injured. You probably were thinking, "This is going to be fun!" You were going to be part of the action.

You've probably had your share of cuts and bruises, scrapes and broken bones just cruising around the neighborhood or skateboarding or playing basketball or football with your friends. Your parents may have taught you safety rules. But now you are older, your body is larger, and your muscle strength is greater. You may not realize that when size and speed increase, the chances of injury also increase.

Now you may be participating in organized sports. If so, you should be pushing yourself to meet greater challenges, and your coach should be showing you the difference between just "knocking around" with your friends and being a trained athlete.

Most of the time participation in organized sports is less risky than just playing around; your school should have the resources to deal with injuries. But the motivation and intensity that you devote to becoming an accomplished athlete should also include conditioning your body and preparing your mind to meet the challenges and deal with risks.

Growth of Sports

In 1991, it was estimated that about 50 percent of boys and 25 percent of girls between the ages of 8 and 16 competed in an organized sports program sometime during the year. People used to think that competitive sports were more suited to boys than to girls, but that view is changing; between 1976 and 1991, female involvement in high school sports is estimated to have increased by 700 percent.

As sports have become increasingly popular with both male and female adolescents, they have also become their second most frequent cause of injury. The National Youth Sports Safety Foundation estimated that more than 5 million children visit hospital emergency rooms each year for treatment of sports injuries—and most of those injuries were from unorganized activities or simple play.

While about 95 percent of sports injuries are minor—bruises, muscle pulls, sprains, strains, and cuts or abrasions—it is estimated that 7 to 10 percent of all spinal injuries occur during sports, especially diving, surfing, and football. Such injuries can range from a neck sprain or pinched nerve to more serious conditions, including paralysis or death.

Growth of Injuries

Any injury can be serious, so how do we explain why so many injuries happen in the first place? Is it because more young men and women participate in sports every year? Or is it because injury prevention is not stressed as part of their program of sports training?

Comparing the increasing numbers of athletes with the number of injuries can be oversimplifying. That is not the only thing to consider. We can ask why 60 percent of all football injuries happen before the first game of the season, while the players are learning to adapt to the demands of the sport. Wouldn't greater concentration on injury prevention, conditioning, and off-season training drastically reduce this statistic? (Chapter 8 discusses this in greater detail.)

No one wants to be one of the thousands of young people who end up frustrated and depressed because of sports injuries. So why do we take the attitude that pain can be tolerated and ignored when common sense tells us that our bodies can take only so much abuse? This attitude contributes to injuries. A lifetime of enjoying your favorite sports can be sacrificed

because "the game" is often considered more important than the players.

Seeking Help

Concentration on learning how your body works
and how to make it work well can make all the difference. When everyone is saying largely, "No pain, no
gain," it takes courage to admit that you're hurting
and need help. Remember, nothing is as important as
your health.

Many factors must be dealt with when you compete
in any sport: your own ambition to excel, awareness
of what your parents and your friends think of you,
steps to condition your body, and the right attitude.
It's a big job. It takes a mature person to do it.

Don't get the idea, however, that all sports injuries
happen at school. Each year about 300,000 children
under 16 are treated in emergency rooms for bike-
related injuries. One in three of those injuries is to the
head, and 85 percent of bike-related deaths are from
head injuries. These statistics prove the importance of
always wearing a helmet when biking. In some places,
helmets are even required by law: Pennsylvania enact-
ed a state law in 1995 requiring all bicyclists under 12
to wear helmets, with fines for the parents of those
who don't obey.

If you follow your doctor's orders, it shouldn't be
long before you're back to your regular routine. It may
seem twice as hard to wait while you recuperate from

Sometimes people try to push their bodies too hard. That's when injuries occur.

some "dumb" accident, but blaming yourself—or anyone else—won't make it any easier.

In the meantime, remember one thing on which the experts agree: You are special. There is no one exactly like you, with your abilities. So don't compare your recovery—or your injuries—with anyone else's. You will recover at your own rate, just as you do everything else.

Chapter 2

Head Injuries

Injuries to the head range from simple bruises and cuts to fractures and brain injuries, including concussion (a violent jolt to the brain). A bruise may cause tenderness, swelling, and discoloration of the skin because the blood vessels under the skin rupture and bleed into underlying tissue. A minor bump on the head should be treated with an ice pack. A bag of frozen vegetables or a plastic bag filled with ice cubes works well; cover it with a towel and apply to the injured spot.

Cuts anywhere on the head, even small ones, may bleed profusely, frightening the victim and those giving first aid. To control bleeding from a cut on the scalp, make a "ring pad" by wrapping a long bandage around all four fingers of your hand, creating a

Head injuries are the most common type of injury.

doughnut-shaped ring. Remove the ring from your hand, position it around the edges of the wound (not directly on it), and apply pressure. If the cut is large or will not stop bleeding, stitches may be needed.

The symptoms of head injuries that require medical care include loss of consciousness; confusion; memory loss; drowsiness; a dent, bruise, or cut on the scalp; severe headache; stiff neck; vomiting; blood or spinal fluid (a clear liquid) coming from the mouth, nose, or ear; changes in vision; pupils of unequal size; convulsions; or the inability to move any part of the body or weakness in an arm or leg. These symptoms may begin right after the injury or may come later, and may indicate a concussion, contusion (a cut or bruising of the brain), or skull fracture.

13

From peewee football to professional baseball, the players of sports wear protective gear.

The Unconscious Patient

Any person who has been "knocked out" by a blow to the head should be treated as if he or she has a back or neck injury. It is extremely important to keep the victim still until professional medical help arrives. Any movement of the head, neck, or back could result in paralysis or death, so do not move the victim unless he or she is in immediate danger—from fire, for example.

Do not remove any protective gear the victim is wearing, including a helmet or shoulder pads. If the victim needs CPR or rescue breathing and is wearing a helmet with a face mask, the face mask should be cut away or unscrewed, leaving the helmet on the victim's head. A person who loses consciousness or experiences any of the symptoms of serious injury (listed above) should receive medical attention as soon as possible.

Danger of Bleeding

Another consequence of head injury is **intracranial bleeding** (bleeding inside the skull or the brain). This can be extremely dangerous and is one of the reasons that *all head injuries should be evaluated immediately by medical personnel.*

Intracranial bleeding is of two types: **arterial** (bleeding from an artery, which causes rapid blood loss) and **subdural** (bleeding from a vein, which is much slower). A person with arterial bleeding may be unconscious briefly, wake for several minutes or even several hours and seem fairly normal, then lose consciousness again and perhaps die if treatment is not prompt. Subdural bleeding is slower and may cause gradual deterioration over several hours or days.

A serious aspect of any head injury is brain swelling, which increases pressure in the skull and can cause unconsciousness, weakness, or paralysis if the nerves affecting the head, neck, and body are involved. Unless dealt with immediately, deterioration can set in and breathing may stop, resulting in possible brain damage and death.

In every case of serious head or neck injury, remember:

- Keep the person calm and quiet until medical help arrives.
- In the case of a less serious injury, get medical care as quickly as possible.
- Give no fluids or food—these could complicate diagnosis or surgery.
- Be prepared to deal with an emergency and know how to get medical help.
- Keep yourself calm and alert.

Chapter 3

Neck Injuries

Some neck injuries are not serious. Even nonathletes can get a stiff neck simply by sleeping in an awkward position. Practicing your serve or throwing a ball can cause fatigue or spasm to the muscles in your neck. When this happens, the best way to get relief is to stretch your neck in the opposite direction.

Strains and sprains of the ligaments of the neck are possible, but rest and use of a cervical collar to support the head and neck will help. Tightness or spasm of the muscle, which occurs when there is bleeding in the muscle and no way for the blood to escape, is a warning of injury.

One type of injury is the **stretching of the neck muscles**. This can happen when you block or hit someone or something with your head, injuring some of the muscles and nerves leading to the shoulders and arms. The pain resembles a series of electric shocks in the neck and arms, and you may experience a weakness in those areas. Permanent weakness can result if the injury is not treated.

Broken Neck

The first seven bones of the spine are called the cervical vertebrae. A break, or fracture, of these bones (usually referred to as a broken neck) is always serious because it could result in damage to the spinal cord and possibly lead to paralysis. Dislocation of the neck (slippage out of normal alignment) does not always involve fracture, but it too can cause permanent damage to the spinal cord.

Whenever a neck injury is suspected, the victim should not be moved unless his or her safety is in immediate danger. For example, from a fire or possible explosion. Extreme caution in the way the victim is handled and prompt treatment for his or her injuries are necessary to prevent further injury and provide the best chance for recovery. If the victim is conscious, be sure that he or she does not try to get up or roll over. Do not the lift the victim's head to place a cushion under it. Use rolled towels or clothing to support the head on both sides, being careful to keep the head, neck, and back perfectly still. If the victim is wearing a hat, helmet, or other protective gear, do not remove it. If the injured person must be moved, one person should hold the victim's head in place with one hand on each side. Do not allow the person's head to move from side to side or to nod up and down. Then, with one person holding the head, several more people should lift the victim onto a stretcher or rigid board, being very careful not to jostle the head, neck, or back.

Breaking your neck is more than just an expression. It's very easy to do if you are hit when your neck is in the wrong position. Many people who land on their head diving into shallow water or being thrown from a horse break their neck. You can break your neck playing football if you hit someone with your head, or someone hits your head, hard enough.

Those seven bones, or vertebrae, can literally explode, causing a dangerous injury; this small area of the backbone is not able to protect the spinal cord as well as it does in the rest of your back. The danger is that when these bones break the spinal cord will tear or separate, causing paralysis.

This is why the head tackle is illegal in college and high school football. Helmets may decrease the danger of head injuries, but remember that your neck is still the weakest point between your helmet and your shoulder pads!

Chapter 4

Back Injuries

A back injury may be as simple as a muscle strain or sprain that requires you to limit activity, or as serious as a direct blow or unusual force to your back, resulting in permanent injury and needing extended therapy.

Young athletes may have a tendency to think that their back is indestructible. And why not? It has taken a lot of abuse and you're still walking around! Let's face it, when you're competing or practicing, with the coach and others watching, you tend to forget how you felt when you woke up this morning. Your neck and legs may have been sore, your back may have ached, and you didn't want to move! You might have been tempted to tell the coach you just couldn't make it today.

The Vulnerable Back

It doesn't take much **strain** or overexertion to

When your coach and the fans are watching you play, it is tempting to try to do just a little more and strain your back.

injure your back, especially if you are already
tired. It's easy to think you can do just a little more
(sports psychologists call this "stinkin' thinkin").
So you try one more set of tennis, one too many
pass blocking drills, or that particular gymnastic
routine. Or you arch your back to strengthen it for
wrestling. Or maybe you try to lift too much
weight, or too much weight too soon—before
you're warmed up. Then your muscles tighten up
and you have strained your back.

Now you are probably lying in pain and
wondering what happened. In all likelihood, you've
torn your muscle fibers and they're bleeding into
the muscle itself. This irritates and inflames the
muscle, which responds by tightening up. Back
muscles are real "monsters"—sometimes up to
two inches thick. And when they tighten up on
you, you'll know it.

When that happens, you're out of commission.
You can't move. An antiinflammatory medication
will help. So will an ice pack, if the pain was
immediate. The cold will help to keep the swelling
down and slow the bleeding.

If the pain came later, heat may help. Stretching
the muscles while sitting in a hot tub could be just
the thing. If you're bending to the left side, stretch
to the right and vice versa.

Ways to Ease Pain

But what if the pain is in your lower back? One

way to stretch, if you can manage it, is to lie down, grab your thighs, and curl up, bending your head and shoulders in. Another way is to slowly bring one leg at a time to your chest.

If the pain is really bad, just lie down and bend your knees; that will move your pelvis up and gently relieve the strain. If that's too painful, try lying on your back with your feet on a pillow.

If you can't bear to lie down, try slowly bending at the waist and coming as close to touching a toe as possible. That will probably feel great, but the trick is straightening up afterward. Try bending your knees first and then straightening up.

The important thing is to do these exercises slowly and consistently, and as soon as possible, to get relief from the spasm and the resulting pain. Do them every ten minutes for a while, then go to twenty, thirty, and so on. Eventually, just stretching before going to bed should be enough. And remember, these same stretching exercises also work well as warm-ups before exercising or competing. When used in this way, they can keep you from re-injuring yourself.

At other times, it may not be a back injury that causes your back pain. Perhaps you bruised your heel on a stone while running. Your natural tendency would be to compensate by walking on the ball of your foot. Your body would adjust to this by twisting itself and sending the back muscles into a spasm.

Self-care begins with the realization of what has

happened to you. You can't fix it until you know what's wrong. Start by stretching your back muscles. Curl-ups should also be done. They are important because they strengthen your stomach muscles, which serve as a stabilizer for your back.

To do this important exercise, lie on your back and rest your hands on your chest. Be sure to keep your knees up and your back flat on the floor. Tilt your pelvis pressing your back flat, then *slowly* curl your head and shoulders up off the floor. Hold, then slowly curl back down. Do about three sets of five if you can. They are tough to do, so don't get discouraged if you can't get up to five. One curl-up equals 15 sit-ups. The important thing is to keep trying. If you do, the benefits will come.

When you're hurting less, you can slowly move into your regular routine. If you continue stretching and strengthening your back and stomach muscles, you'll help prevent a recurrence.

Knowing Your Limits

It is also important to know your limits, because one of these days your back may send signals that say, "This is serious! It's time to consult your doctor." Pay attention to these warnings:

- Back pain that goes into your arm, leg, or groin
- Numbness, tingling, or strange sensations in your arms or legs

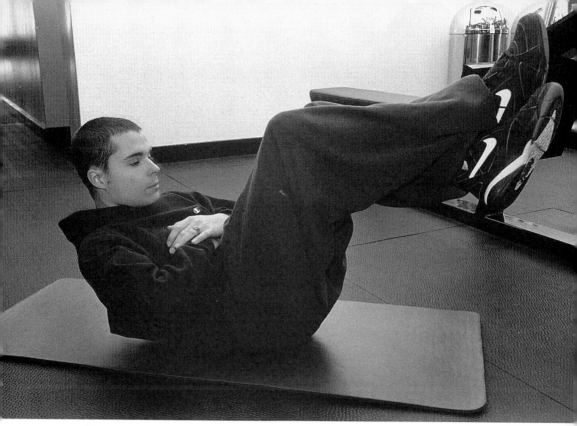

Sit-ups, curl-ups, or crunches strengthen your stomach, which then helps relieve stress and pressure on your back.

- Weakness in your arms or legs
- Coughing, sneezing, or other straining—like a bowel movement—that makes the pain worse

If you experience any of these symptoms, you could have an injury that involves nerve damage. If so, consult your doctor immediately! It makes no difference whether an injury is sudden or the result of overuse; these symptoms may indicate that your spinal column has been damaged, which is among the most dangerous injuries you can have.

Slipped Disk

Another type of back injury is one that involves

the **disks**. Your backbone runs from the bottom of your head to your tailbone. It contains over 30 separate vertebrae (bones) connected by ligaments, with disks between the vertebrae. Your spinal cord runs down the center of your backbone. It sends signals back and forth between your brain and your body. The disks are like spacers that absorb shock between the bones. The outside of the disks is tough, and the inside is gelatin-like.

When you have an injury that moves one of these little shock absorbers, the disk may move to one side or it may lose some of its fluid and become stiff. This is called a ruptured or slipped disk. The damaged disk may put pressure on the spinal cord, causing severe pain and loss of nerve function. It may even affect bladder or bowel control. It could cause permanent paralysis.

Treatment for a disk problem ranges from complete rest to medication to deal with inflammation and swelling. When all else fails, it may be necessary to remove a damaged disk surgically. This is called a laminectomy.

Stress Fracture

One back problem that results from overuse or misuse is a **stress fracture** (small, hairline break). This injury seems to result from overarching the back. Gymnasts may incur this injury during a dismount, and football linemen can get it coming out of position to block. It can also happen anytime the backbone is compressed as in pole vaulting, weight lifting, or jumping on a trampoline.

Once again, the simplest solution can be straightening your backbone and strengthening your stomach muscles. These fractures usually heal themselves with a long rest.

Another back injury is a **contusion** (result of a direct blow that causes blood vessels to bleed into the muscle). These injuries are common among football players. They usually happen when a player is hit with a knee, an elbow, or a helmet or is knocked on his back. They are treated in the same way as neck contusions (see above).

The main thing to remember about back injuries is to catch them early and pay attention to pain. Pain is the way your body tells you to stop and take care of yourself. It's not weakness—it's just good sense. Find out what's happening and take care of the problem!

Chapter 5

Arm, Shoulder, and Hand Injuries

Playing any of the throwing games—baseball, basketball, football, even bowling—requires us to move our arms, elbows, wrists, and shoulders in the same way over and over. No wonder so many injuries affect those parts of the body. Besides the sports mentioned, we play hockey, golf, racquetball, and tennis. We also lift weights, swim, ride bikes, row boats, and do gymnastics. Each repetitive movement can set us up for injury—and falls and blows can cause injury to these sensitive areas.

Your shoulders, arms, wrists, and elbows are the most flexible parts of your body. While this enables you make the movements required to dress, it also makes it easy to injure these body parts—and life after such an injury is frustrating. Simple things like combing your hair, brushing your teeth, or just getting dressed can be a problem.

Because of the flexibility of joints such as the shoulders and wrists, it is easier to injure these body parts.

Tennis Elbow

The single biggest factor in sports injuries is the way we use our muscles. Our muscles come in pairs, and we usually overuse one set while underusing the other. The kind of injury people get depends on which set they use in the sport they play.

An example is **tennis elbow**—the result of the backhand stroke used in playing tennis. When you use your wrist without using the rest of your arm, the strain on your wrist muscles is often too much; it may cause the other end of those muscles, attached to the inside of the elbow, to become inflamed, torn, or separated.

A similar injury is **Little League elbow**. In children and youths, the muscles on the inside of the elbow are not very strong. One hard throw can injure them.

These injuries take quite a while to heal. Usually, antiinflammatory medication, ice, and rest will help. Strengthening exercises help to prevent a repeat injury. Using equipment with larger grips and less weight will also help. It is equally important to learn to throw properly and only when necessary.

Forearm, wrist, and hand injuries can be serious and should be treated by your doctor. They may require x-rays, splints, and casts. Do not try to ignore the pain and swelling. Don't try to treat yourself. Injuries can include fractures (broken bones), carpal tunnel syndrome, nerve compression, contusions, and sprains. As usual, ice, antiinflammatory medication, and rest (for up to six weeks) are the best treatments.

Carpal Tunnel Syndrome

With an injury like **carpal tunnel syndrome** or **carpal tunnel fracture**, failure to seek medical attention could leave you permanently injured. Numbness or tingling of the first three fingers can be a sign that you have this type of injury. It is caused by overuse of your hand and wrist and is treated with medication, splints, exercise, and temporarily stopping the activity that caused the injury. If this doesn't work, surgery may be necessary.

If the numbness or tingling is in your fourth and fifth fingers, you may have injured your "**funny bone**" or overused your wrist. Called an **ulnar nerve compression**, it is treated with rest and by switching to better equipment.

Although a sprained finger or wrist may need to be x-rayed, taped, or put in a splint, a dislocated finger may take longer to heal to avoid permanent damage.

Contact Sport Injuries

Shoulder and upper arm injuries are a hazard in

all contact sports. For instance, football and hockey players can experience a shoulder separation because of stretched or torn ligaments connecting the shoulder to the collarbone. A shoulder separation (partial tear) can heal in a few days by putting the arm in a sling. A complete separation usually requires surgery.

Baseball players and fans have heard of the torn or inflamed **rotator cuff** that pitchers suffer. The rotator cuff is a set of three muscles that hold together the **humerus** (the main bone of the shoulder) and the **scapula** (shoulder blade).

Surprising to most athletes, the shoulder joint is like a golf ball resting against a small saucer. The only thing holding it there is a few muscles and tendons. That's why shoulders are so easy to twist and swing—and why they're so easy to injure. When your shoulder is out of commission, you're not only out of the tennis match, track meet, or basketball game, you're suddenly out of all your daily activities—even opening doors, buttoning shirts, lacing shoes, or lifting a glass to your mouth.

One of the most common shoulder injuries is a broken **clavicle** (collarbone). This can be caused by a direct blow or by reaching out to break a fall. The clavicle is not much thicker than a finger bone. It will hurt like crazy and swell, but after it's set, it should heal.

Contusions to the shoulder are seldom serious.

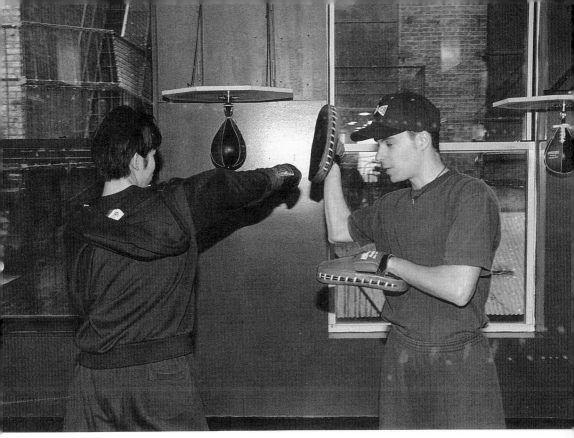

Sports such as boxing are more strenuous on certain parts of the body, like the shoulders.

They usually affect the **deltoid muscle** (the big muscle that caps your shoulder and protects the other muscles and tendons). If the deltoid muscle goes into spasm, you will overuse other muscles. This will cause you to learn new, unhealthy ways of playing your sport. These habits will be hard to break when your shoulder is well again. Another problem is that those substitute muscles won't be as strong, and further injury could be the result.

Strains

Strains are another common injury. When the **rhomboids** (muscles in the center of your back that hold the edge of your shoulder blade to your spine) go into spasm, you'll have little knots in the center of your back that are hard and painful. Help it by resting the muscle. You can also stretch it by "hugging" yourself, and strengthen it by leaning forward and folding your arms like wings and flapping them backwards.

If the **trapezius** (the big muscle that runs down your back to your waistline) goes into spasm, rest for a couple of hours. Then start stretching and strengthening it. Shoulder shrugs are a good way to do that.

A strain of the **triceps** (the muscle on the outside of your upper arm) is usually the result of overuse, usually from doing clean-and-jerk weight lifting, throwing, or hitting backhands. Resting from your sport, using ice, and correcting your form can lead to recovery.

Chapter 6

Leg and Knee Injuries

If your sport is track or basketball, you already know the importance of your legs and their muscles. Most leg injuries can be avoided by warming up, thereby avoiding running on your toes and preventing overuse.

Remember that overuse can be a result of favoring one muscle over another, but overuse injuries can also happen because of change. A change in stride, distance, speed, terrain, surface, or shoes can be enough to cause overuse injuries. So can returning too quickly to your sport after being sick. Because muscles deteriorate quickly, they must be reconditioned before full-fledged competition.

Importance of Prevention

Prevention is the key here. Since tightness in the calf is a common leg problem, try this stretching exercise several times a day: Put your palms on the wall and your heels flat on the floor about thirty inches from the wall; with your knees and arms straight, push your stomach to the wall.

Your lower leg has two bones, the **tibia** (the largest bone in the lower leg, which supports 80 to 90 percent of your body's weight), and the **fibula** (the smaller of the two bones in the lower leg). The leg muscles are divided by thick tissue into compartments. Those are called the anterior, superior, posterior, deep posterior, and lateral.

Acute compartmental syndrome is the name given to pain or injury of these muscles, and it's almost always serious. When the muscles swell, blood flow to these compartments is restricted. It may take major surgery to correct this. The best thing to do is stop running before it gets that bad. Severe pain with tingling and numbness are present when you move your ankle or toes. If you have enlarged leg muscles and gradual pain while running, you probably have **chronic compartmental syndrome**, which may respond to a lower level of activity or may require surgery to relieve the pressure.

Your doctor may diagnose **deep posterior compartmental syndrome** by measuring pressure in the compartment with a Wick Catheter. The pain may last for several hours after exercising and be accompanied by tingling and numbness. Surgery will be required. **Stress**

fractures are something else not to be ignored. They show up when you're pulling on your sock and notice pain.

Stress Fractures

If you can spot tenderness when you run your finger down your shin but nothing shows up on an x-ray, you may have stress fracture (the bone has bent almost to breaking and has a hairline crack in it).

This can also result from a change in your routine or activity. Your bones react to force or stress in an odd manner. As you increase the stress on a bone, new bone doesn't simply grow on top of the old. Instead, the bone starts removing old bone so that new bone can grow. This means that the bone is not as strong as it would be normally.

Before things get serious, find a level of activity as heavy but as pain-free as possible. In this way, you'll be conditioning the bone to heal so it will be ready when you resume your original level of activity. Go slow and don't push too far. It takes time for bone to disappear and rejuvenate. Three weeks into recovery, you should slow down for ten to fourteen days.

True fractures are something you can't treat yourself. But be sure that your doctor gives you good rehabilitation exercises (so you won't come out of the cast with stiff, useless legs).

Shin Splints

Shin splints occur when muscles pull away from the **shinbone**. You'll know you've got them if the area hurting is about twelve inches long on the front part of your lower leg. Treatment is a matter of trial and error, including taping the leg, using arch supports or heel inserts, applying ice, and taking antiinflammatory medication. Strengthening and stretching the lower leg muscles is one of the first things to do. Try attaching some rubber tubing to a board, putting your foot on the board, then pulling the tubing upward with your arms and hands. Your toes should curl slightly downward. Change the slack in the tubing as stretching increases, and do some calf stretching before and after.

Knee Injuries

The knee is involved in more than 25 percent of all sports injuries and 75 percent of those requiring surgery. An engineering miracle, the knee is flexible enough to bend 150 degrees front to back, about 4 degrees to the side, and to rotate 90 degrees. It withstands pressures up to 2,000 pounds and is self-lubricating.

The knees are the source of so many injuries because they are subjected to a lot of abuse. Although they are large joints, many things can go wrong with so much bone, the thickest **cartilage** in the body, seven separate **ligaments**, one huge **tendon** and several smaller ones, and many **bursa** (sac-like cavities between joints).

Boys between the ages of 10 and 14 are especially prone to two kinds of knee injuries. The first type of injury is called **Osgood-Schlatter**. Although the cause of it is not certain, overuse is usually a factor. This results in a pulling on the kneecap tendon, which causes the near end of the tibia (the front bone in the lower leg) to fragment at the point where the tendon attaches. When the knee is bent, pain develops just below the patella (kneecap). This makes you want to walk and run with a stiff leg. The condition clears up on its own with rest, limited exercise, and protective knee pads.

The second injury is called **osteochondritis dessicans**, which is as hard to pronounce as it to put up with. Symptoms include pain, swelling, a lump over the knee, and knee-locking. When the knee gets knocked around enough, a part of the bone inside dies and the cartilage over the knee separates and falls into the joint. Depending on how early it is diagnosed, your doctor may recommend immobilization (locking the knee permanently) or surgery to remove the cartilage.

Overuse of Muscles

Although you may be tired of hearing about overuse as a cause of injury, many athletes do

overuse their bodies and pay the price for doing
so. Tendinitis, bursitis, and synovitis are three
more examples of overuse. While they can be
caused by a blow to the knee, most doctors
believe they are usually caused by too much use
too soon—too much running, kicking, and
exercise.

With **tendinitis**, you'll find that rest, ice, and
antiinflammatory medication will help relieve the
pain and tenderness. You will aggravate it if you
continue to exercise—and you will hear a grinding
noise whenever you do. Sprinters and weight
lifters may get tendinitis in the quadriceps (the
large muscle on the front of the upper leg).
Athletes who jump too much can get it in the
patella (kneecap)—called "jumper's knee." Long-
distance runners get it in the hamstring (the large
muscle at the back of the upper leg).

Tenderness and a grating sensation along with
swelling may mean **bursitis**, an inflammation of
the bursa (a small sac filled with lubricating liquid
that reduces the friction between tendons and
bones). Bursitis can become chronic (permanent)
if the knee is abused long enough. The
result is heavy-duty pain and swelling. The best
treatment is drainage and an injection of cortisone.
Basketball players and athletes who fall on
artificial turf may get **prepatellar bursitis**
(swelling in the sac under the kneecap). This will
probably need to be drained by medical personnel.

On the other hand, wearing protective pads can usually prevent the injury.

Synovitis is swelling and inflammation of the membrane lining the knee joint. If this condition becomes serious, you will probably need to see an orthopedic surgeon. An **arthroscope** is a tiny telescope with a light and video camera that is inserted into the knee through a 1/4-inch cut. This is a very expensive operation and may not be necessary if your doctor thinks that rehabilitation and treatment could take care of your problem.

Another thing to consider is that after surgery you may never get back to your original level. You may lose 10 percent or more of your playing ability. Surgery is always a risk, no matter how miraculous it may seem. Remember, a Joe Montana may come back after surgery and seem to play as well as he ever did. But he started out better than the average player, he makes his living playing, and he's aware of the trade-offs—like future problems. High school athletes don't get the same kind of medical attention, and they don't get an around-the-clock personal trainer, either! Also, you may not be willing to spend up to half your time in rehabilitation for six to ten months after surgery.

Sprained ligaments can be caused by sudden turning of the knee or a violent twist of the body after a lower leg blow. The sprain may be mild, or involve a complete rupture of the **medial**

It is important to stretch the hamstrings and calves before exercising.

meniscus (a disk that cushions bone in a joint). Mild cases can be treated with ice and rest, but severe cases require a cast or surgery.

Whether caused by wear and tear, sudden twisting, or a blow to the knee, either of the two cartilages can be torn. The symptoms are pain or swelling, locking, or popping sounds in the knee. In this case, you will need to see an orthopedic surgeon for diagnosis and treatment.

Dislocated Kneecap

A dislocated kneecap is a very painful injury. It can be caused by a fall, weak ligaments around the kneecap, or a blow to the knee. If you dislocate a kneecap, you will not be able to straighten your leg. There will be a bulge on the side of your knee. Your doctor will put a cast or splint on it to allow it to heal, and with luck you won't need surgery. If you break a kneecap, you will notice swelling in the knee and a crunching feeling. An x-ray will be needed to confirm the fracture. If so, your orthopedic surgeon will take it from there.

He or she might recommend strengthening exercises to condition your leg. A weighted shoe, weighing about five pounds, would be as effective as a gym machine.

In the upper leg, the **femur** (thighbone that runs from the hip to the knee) is the longest and strongest bone in your body. The muscles (quadriceps in front and hamstring in back—also called the **adductor** and **abductor**) move your hips and knee joints.

The **quadriceps** is your body's most powerful muscle. It gives you power and speed. The three hamstring muscles straighten your hips and bend your knees. They are very important for runners.

Running

Runners remember: Beware overdeveloping your quadriceps and neglecting your hamstrings— you may find yourself with pulled muscles. The next time you run, they will put you in severe pain. When that happens, don't continue to run! If you do, you'll end up with bleeding muscles. For hamstrings, you should try a compression wrap, ice, massage, and gentle stretching for a few days. For quadriceps, you may need to do this for three weeks. Later, rest and heat could help both. It will take about six weeks to recover completely.

A **charley horse** is a muscle contusion or bruise that usually involves the quadriceps. A running back can get one from being tackled. If the bruising is bad, the muscles swell and the knees lose range of movement. Bruising causes muscle tightness and pain when the muscle cools down. You may have to treat it with ice and a compression wrap and rest for a day or two. You may also need to wear a hard thigh pad for protection. And when you get back on the field, don't push yourself.

Sometimes, after a really bad contusion, you may get **myositis ossificans** (bones forming in the muscle and connecting tissue). This can cause a great deal of pain and swelling, and often lasts for weeks at a time. You will need to rely on your doctor's advice and do only as much as you can bear. Exercise and massage won't help. At the worst, you may have three to six months of disability.

If you notice pain along the side of your knee that doesn't ease when you are running and a noticeable tightness all along your thigh, you may have a tight **iliotibial band** (the strongest and longest ligament in your body). Rest, ice, and antiinflammatory medication should help. A wrap won't help—and could make it worse. Stretching exercises can help prevent recurrence.

Overdoing running on hard surfaces can result in stress fracture of the **femur** (the thigh bone). Don't ignore this, because it can become a complete fracture. Immediate treatment is needed. It can be an emergency because of serious blood loss and shock, as well as major swelling and pain. A bone scan (instead of an x-ray) can confirm the injury. Rest for about six weeks usually helps.

Chapter 7

Hernias

A hernia (a bulge of soft tissue that forces its way through or between muscles) is not usually as serious as some people think. Weak or torn muscles allow the tissue to push out. The only symptom is usually swelling, which can form slowly over several weeks, or suddenly while lifting a heavy weight. You may feel a tenderness, or perhaps a "dragging" or heaviness.

Hernias are most common in the abdominal wall (muscles and fat that cover the stomach, intestines, liver, and kidneys). The most common type for athletes is an **inguinal hernia** (one that occurs in the groin). Some hernias can be pushed back into place with no problem. If not, your doctor will probably recommend surgery to take out the hernia sac and shorten or bring together the weak muscles. He or she will also tell you to take it easy for about a month and do no heavy lifting.

If a hernia involves the intestine, the contents of the intestine will not be able to pass through and you will have pain, nausea, and vomiting. This is called an **obstructed hernia**. If the hernia swells and cuts off the blood supply to the intestine, the strangulated hernia becomes red, extremely painful, and enlarged. It requires emergency surgery.

Other types of hernias include **femoral** (upper thigh), **epigastric** (centered just below the breasts), and **paraumbilical** (belly-button). The important thing to remember is that most hernias can get worse. The danger, especially with a groin hernia, is that intestinal strangulation will occur. Surgery and following your doctor's orders will get you back on your feet as soon as possible.

Chapter 8

Preventing Sports Injuries

Preventing sports injuries is one of the most important things any athlete will ever do. Any professional athlete will tell you the same thing, "You can't play if you aren't well!" By now, you know that thousands of athletes your age are injured every year. Before you become one of them, or become one of them again, read and apply the principles in this chapter. They work!

Injury prevention includes conditioning, training, performing—and a whole lot more! Being in shape is great. So is understanding your sport. Does that mean you're ready to go out there and show them your stuff? Not yet!

Condition Your Body for Your Sport

Far too many athletes who are in excellent shape are injured every year. Sometimes it's because they didn't take conditioning seriously. Conditioning means getting your body in shape *for your particular sport*. It takes very different approaches to condition your body for the games of football, basketball, and baseball. The reason? Each sport makes very different demands on your body.

Conditioning for football and gymnastics are as different as the rules for each sport. When you understand conditioning as a way of being ready, you have accepted the idea that you have to be physically able to answer the demands your sport makes on you. Some sports require explosive, short bursts of energy, whereas others require endurance. Football players can "run" several plays in an hour-long game with a lot of short rests, but few if any could run a marathon.

"Appropriate" conditioning means not only that you're able to compete successfully, but that the program is right for you at your stage of growth. An overintensive conditioning program can get you injured before you ever have a chance to compete.

Good conditioning workouts build stamina *and* endurance, strength *and* muscle tone. You should gain greater agility *and* flexibility, better coordination *and* balance. Where you start depends on what your physical and emotional limits are at your age.

Condition from Your Baseline

Remember, all great athletes condition. They start by finding out what they are able to do, *now*. This is called an "athlete's personal baseline" (APB). It is their own personal starting point. Professional athletes know better than to start training at someone else's baseline.

Imagine a professional athlete being stupid enough to start lifting at Walter Thomas's baseline? Walter may be the world's greatest power lifter. His record 2,050 pounds in three lifts—squat, bench, and dead lift—may never be broken. A fool who tried to start lifting at such a level—would end up with a crushed chest, a broken back, and all his leg muscles ripped loose. So all athletes must find their APB.

Then they *gradually* increase the level and intensity of their workouts. This is the principle of *progressive differentiation*. If you want to run ten miles and your APB is one mile, try running one and a half miles. When you've mastered that, run two miles. Your success depends on you—your ability, your maturity, and your commitment—and on realistic, reasonable goals that are right for you.

Plan Your Workout

You need to plan your workout. Divide each one into four parts: warm-up, skills practice, sport-related practice, and cool-down. The warm-up increases blood flow to your muscles and stretches your tissues for maximum flexibility. Fifteen minutes of vigorous exercise raises muscle temperature to about 103 degrees, which warms up all the major muscle groups in the legs, arms, back, hips, and torso.

Because most sports have specific skills, this is the main part of your workout. Don't concentrate on more than one or two skills in each workout. If your sport is one that does not require several skills, then speed, distance, or endurance will be what you work on.

Next, spend a few minutes actually playing your sport. It makes little difference whether you call this phase "scrimmage," "practice match," "volleying," or "batting practice." The point is, all athletes get turned on and tuned in by playing their sport. Without this component in your training program, you won't feel enthusiastic or focused. And that's dangerous. Athletes who are bored or distracted are candidates for injury.

Then it is time for the cool-down phase of training. This should last about 15 minutes. You should slow down but continue exercising—a brisk walk, gentle calisthenics, or cycling at a moderate pace are good cool-down exercises. Then hit the showers—warm is best, by the way.

The final step is just as important as the warm-up. After working out, your muscles should be tight. They need to be stretched and gently

exercised to get rid of the excess lactic acid
(which enters the blood with adrenaline during
exercise and signals an increase in heart rate).

One thing is common to all training: If you
do it right, you'll have less risk of injury. The
various injuries are specific to certain sports, and a
good training program will help prevent them. If
you're not sure your training is doing that, ask
your coach, trainer, or a sports medicine
specialist.

Train for Endurance and Power

There are two types of muscles: slow-twitch and
fast-twitch. If you have a lot of fast-twitch or fast-
firing muscles, you'll do better in sports that need
speed and intense power with short bursts of
energy. If you have more slow-twitch muscles,
sports that require endurance are best for you.
That doesn't mean that you should train only one
set of muscles. Endurance and speed are both
important in most sports, so your conditioning
should include aerobic exercise and anaerobic
training.

Understanding your body's energy-producing
ability means knowing something about its two
types of metabolism: increasing *aerobic metabolic
capacity* is the goal of endurance training. This
type of metabolism depends on oxygen to convert
energy. It is the type of training you should be

doing if your sport is long-distance running, bicycle racing, or basketball. You want to do things to train your body to have more endurance. Good exercises would be dance aerobics, running, swimming laps, speed-walking. If weights are used, you'll do weight lifting with lots of repetitions.

On the other hand, fuel for *anaerobic metabolism* is stored in the muscle fiber. This means that bursts of energy are produced that result in explosive activity. One goal of anaerobic exercise is training the muscles to resist the presence of lactic acid. A build-up of this chemical happens fast with high-intensity exercise, causing fatigue and muscle discomfort. Sports such as football, shot-putting, and power lifting are typical of this kind of metabolism. You need to include things like heavy weight lifting and sprinting in your training program.

Weight Train Sensibly

If weight training is a part of your training program, keep a few things in mind. Most weight lifting equipment is not made for people your age. Ten pounds can be too much of an increase for a new lifter. And increasing your lifts in large increments can set you up for injury by forcing you to develop bad lifting habits in trying to compensate. If you are a beginning lifter, you will need more supervision and instruction than friends who are more seasoned lifters.

Make sure the person teaching you to lift isn't fanatical. Some people think weight lifting is all there is to life! Don't let a fanatic push you too hard, making you attempt to lift weights you're not ready to lift. Trying to lift too much too soon can seriously damage your body, ripping apart bones, ligaments, cartilage, and muscles—sometimes permanently! And remember the basic rules for weight lifting:

1. Always warm up. (Weights are notorious for damaging cold muscles).
2. Stretch after lifting. (If you don't, you will become "muscle-bound," losing so much range of motion that you won't be able to move well.)
3. Never lift without a "spotter" (someone to help if you get into trouble during a lift—all pro lifters use one).
4. Only lift weight you can control (quivering means you're lifting too much).
5. Lift deliberately and come down the same way.
6. Work up to heavier weights gradually (remember the principle of progressive differentiation).
7. Use equipment that's the right size—or as close to the right size as possible—for you.
8. Don't hurry a lift (forced = loss of control).

9. Never lift two days in a row—alternate with aerobic workouts every other day.
10. Never arch your back, especially during the bench press.
11. BREATHE! Breathe out when you lift—"blow" the weight up—and breathe in as you bring the weight down to the starting position. (Holding your breath while straining to lift will dramatically increase your blood pressure and you could have a stroke or heart attack).
12. Don't ignore pain, especially in the joints. (If it is severe, or if it lasts more than a couple of days, stop lifting and see your team trainer or doctor immediately.)

Eat Like an Athlete

What you eat every day has a lot to do with how well you can compete and how well you can resist injuries. A longstanding myth had everyone thinking athletes really have to "chow down" before the "big game." Don't buy this. Eating too much before competing can be disastrous. A large part of your body's energy may be needed to digest the meal, leaving you feeling sluggish.

Most athletes relax before competing in order to conserve energy. What's important is to eat a balanced diet of high-energy and nutritious foods. The best sources for the calories you need are grains, dried fruits, breads, and pastas. These

Eating healthy foods helps keep your body in its best form.

foods, called "complex carbohydrates," are important because they contain minerals and glycogen. When you exercise, glycogen converts to glucose to make fuel for your muscles.

What happens when your muscles burn glucose? It forms a compound called pyruvate, which combines with oxygen to form carbon dioxide and water, which the lungs excrete. When the exercise is intense and strenuous, pyruvate changes to lactic acid because there's not enough oxygen. Your lungs can't get rid of that, the muscles won't contract, and you slow down. Even well-trained athletes can reach the point where their body can't get enough oxygen to the muscles, but they know when to slow down.

And don't forget to drink enough water. Dehydration causes lower muscle strength and cuts your level of glycogen.

There are no "magic" diets or vitamins that will improve your performance or guarantee you a successful career equal to that of your favorite sports star. In fact, certain vitamins or minerals can be dangerous if you take too much of them (vitamins A and D and iron are all poisonous in large amounts, and too much niacin can damage your heart). And never eat sugar-laden food during competition; it won't give you extra energy or strength, but it will force the blood into your stomach and intestines and may cause you to lose the competitive edge.

Protective Equipment

There is one basic rule about protective equipment: *Use what is appropriate for your sport.* Watch sport professionals in actual competition. You'll see batters wearing helmets, football players wearing everything from shoulder pads to face guards, basketball players wearing knee pads and protective goggles.

Why do you think the best players—many of them earning at least a million dollars a year— wear protective equipment? They got where they are by using their heads, and they want to live long enough to enjoy spending those millions!

Glossary

abdominal wall Muscles and fat that cover the stomach, intestines, liver, and kidneys.

abductor The muscle on the back of the thigh, running from the buttocks to the knee; also called the *hamstring*.

adductor The body's largest muscle, on the front and outside of the upper leg; also called *quadriceps*.

adrenaline Chemical that causes the body to become excited, increasing heart rate, blood pressure, energy level, and awareness.

arterial bleeding Bleeding from an artery, usually a large flow of blood.

arthroscope Tiny telescope with a light and video camera attached, used by orthopedic surgeons.

athlete's personal baseline Each athlete's point at which to begin training.

atrophy Process by which a body part dries up and becomes useless.

bursa Sac-like cavities between joints.

bursitis Inflammation of the bursa due to overuse.

carpal tunnel syndrome Pain in wrist and numbing of the first three fingers due to overuse.

cartilage Tough, elastic tissue that forms a part of the skeleton.

cervical vertebrae First seven bones of the spine, located in the neck.

chronic compartmental syndrome Dangerous condition that results in restricted blood flow in the lower leg muscles.

clavicle The collarbone.

concussion Violent jolt to the brain.

complex carbohydrates Energy foods such as bread, pasta, and dried fruits.

contusion Result of a direct blow that causes: (1) bruising of the brain, or (2) rupture of blood vessels and bleeding into a muscle.

disks Spacers that hold the vertebrae apart.

fast-twitch muscles Muscles that enable the athlete to have short, powerful bursts of energy.

femoral hernia Hernia of the upper thigh.

glucose Body sugar that combines with oxygen to form an essential part of the energy chain.

hernia Bulge of soft tissue that forces its way through or between muscles.

intracranial bleeding Bleeding inside the skull or brain.

lactic acid Chemical that builds up in muscles during and after exercise, making the muscles sore.

laminectomy Surgical removal of a disk from the backbone.

medial meniscus Disk that cushions bones in joints.

obstructed hernia Hernia that swells to the point that the contents of the intestines are blocked. Can lead to *strangulated hernia.*

Osgood-Schlatter disease Pulling of the kneecap tendon, which causes the tibia to fragment where the tendon attaches.

prepatellar bursitis Bursitis of the sac under the kneecap.

progressive differentiation The way in which athletes achieve training and recovery goals in small increments.

rotator cuff Set of three muscles that hold the humerus and scapula together.

shin splints Pain resulting from muscle pulling away from the lower front leg bone.

slow-twitch muscles Muscles that enable an athlete to have greater levels of endurance.

stress fracture Fine, hairline break of a bone.

subdural bleeding Bleeding from a vein; usually a very slow blood flow.

synovitis Inflammation and swelling of the membrane lining the knee joint.

tendinitis Overuse of the tendons causing inflammation and swelling.

trapezius Large muscle that runs down the back to the waist.

triceps Muscles that run down the outside of the upper arm.

vertebrae The approximately thirty bones that make up the backbone.

Where to Go for Help

Avoiding Injury

The best people to talk to about avoiding sports injuries are your physical education teacher, coach, trainer, or doctor. They are all trained in teaching people how to avoid injury. Your parents may also be able to help you develop and stick to an exercise program that will strengthen the muscles you need for your sport.

Dealing with Drinking and Drug Use

If you or a friend are using alcohol, steroids, or other drugs, there are many ways for you to receive free, confidential information and assistance. Groups such as Alcoholics Anonymous (AA) and Narcotics Anonymous (NA) exist to help people with concerns about alcohol and drug use. There is also special assistance available for children whose parents are substance abusers, through groups such as Al-Anon and Nar-Anon. You may call 1-800-ALCOHOL (1-800-252-6465) for information on programs and hotlines near you, or look in your area phone book for local groups.

Alcohol Hotline
(800) ALCOHOL (252-6465)

American Council for Drug Education
204 Monroe Street
Rockville, MD 20850

Narcotics Anonymous
(818) 780-3951

For Further Reading

Bar-Or, Oded, editor. *The Child and Adolescent Athlete*. Cambridge, MA: Blackwell Science, 1995.

Betz, Randal R., editor. *Child with a Spinal Cord Injury*. Rosemont, IL: American Academy of Orthopedic Surgeons, 1996.

Hawkins, Jerald D. *Sports Medicine: A Practical Guide for Youth Sports, Coaches and Parents*. Canton, OH: Professional Reports Corp, 1992.

Lukas, Scott E. *Steroids*. Springfield, NJ: Enslow Publishers, 1994.

Micheli, Lyle J., and Mark D. Jenkins, *Sportswise: An Essential Guide for Young Athletes, Parents and Coaches*. Boston: Houghton Mifflin, 1990.

Reider, Bruce, editor. *Sports Medicine: The School-Age Athlete*. Philadelphia: W. B. Saunders Co., 1996.

Sullivan, J. Andy. *Pediatric Athlete*. Rosemont, IL: American Academy of Orthopedic Surgeons, 1990.

Index

A

antiinflammatory medication, 22, 30, 31, 38, 40, 45

arm, shoulder, and hand injuries, 9, 28–34

arthoscope, 41

athlete's personal baseline (APB), 50–51

B

back injuries, 20–27

baseball, 28, 32

basketball, 28, 32, 35, 40, 53

brain injury, 15–16

broken neck, 18–19

bruises, 12, 44

bursitis, 40

C

carpal tunnel syndrome, 31

charley horse, 44

clavicle, broken, 32

compartment syndrome, 36

concussion, 10, 12–13

conditioning, 48–51

contact sport injuries, 31–33

contusion, 27, 31, 32, 44

cool-down, 52

D

deltoid muscle, 33

diet, 56–58

dislocation, neck, 18

E

exercise, 22–24, 30, 31, 36, 37, 40, 53

F

femoral hernia, 47

femur, 43–44, 45

fibula, 36

football, 9–10, 27, 28, 32, 49, 54

fractures, 9, 18, 30–31, 43

G

gymnastics, 22, 26, 28, 49

H

hamstring, 40

head injuries, 12–16

help, seeking, 10

hernia, 46–47

humerus, 32

I

iliotibial band, 45

inguinal hernia, 46–47

injuries, growth of, 9–10

K

knee injuries, 38–39

L

laminectomy, 26

leg and knee injuries, 9, 35–45

M

medial meniscus, 41–43

63

metabolism, aerobic/anaerobic, 53
myositis ossificans, 45

N
neck injuries, 9, 17–19

O
Osgood–Schlatter injury, 39
osteochondritis dessicans, 39
overuse, muscle, 39–43

P
pain
    as warning, 10, 22, 24–25, 27, 30,
        36, 39, 40, 44, 55
    ways to ease, 22–24
paralysis, 16, 26
patella, dislocated, 39, 40, 43–44
prevention, injury, 9–10, 35–37,
    48–58

Q
quadriceps, 40, 44

R
recovery, length of, 30, 44, 45
rhomboid muscles, 33–34
rotator cuff, 32
running, 35, 36, 40, 44–45, 53

S
scapula, 32

shin splints, 38
shoulder separation, 32
slipped disk, 25–26
spinal cord, 18, 26
sprains, 9, 17, 20, 31, 41
strains, 9, 17, 20, 33–34
stress fracture, 26–27, 36–37, 45
surgery, 16, 26, 31, 36, 39, 41, 43, 46,
    47
synovitis, 40–41

T
tendinitis, 40
tennis, 22, 28, 32
tennis elbow, 30
training, endurance and power,
    52–54
trapezius muscle, 34

U
ulnar nerve compression, 31
unconsciousness, 13–16, 18

V
vertebrae, 18, 26

W
warm–ups, 23, 51, 54
weight lifting, 22, 27, 28, 40, 50–51,
    53–55
workout, planning, 51–52

About the Author

Dr. Lawrence Clayton earned his doctorate from Texas Woman's University. He is an ordained minister and has served as such since 1972. Dr. Clayton is a clinical marriage and family therapist and certified drug and alcohol counselor. He is also president of the Oklahoma Professional Drug and Alcohol Counselors Certification Board. Dr. Clayton lives with his wife, Cathy, and their three children in Piedmont, Oklahoma.

Photo Credits

Cover by Lauren Piperno; pp. 2, 13 by Kim Sonsky; pp. 6, 11, 25, 29, 33, 42 by Michael Brandt; pp. 21, 56 by Marcus Shaffer; p. 14 © AP/Wide World Photo.